PAUL ROMANUK

HOCKEY SUPERSTARS

2015-2016

Your complete guide to the 2015–2016 season,
featuring action photos of
your favorite players

SCHOLASTIC

TORONTO NEW YORK LONDON AUCKLAND SYDNEY
MEXICO CITY NEW DELHI HONG KONG BUENOS AIRES

THE TEAMS

CALGARY FLAMES
team colors: red, gold, black and white
home arena: Scotiabank Saddledome
mascot: Harvey the Hound
Stanley Cups won: 1

. . . .

EDMONTON OILERS
team colors: white, royal blue and orange
home arena: Rexall Place
Stanley Cups won: 5

. . . .

ANAHEIM DUCKS
team colors: black, gold, orange and white
home arena: Honda Center
mascot: Wild Wing
Stanley Cups won: 1

LOS ANGELES KINGS
team colors: white, black and silver
home arena: Staples Center
mascot: Bailey
Stanley Cups won: 2

. . . .

ARIZONA COYOTES
team colors: red, black, sand and white
home arena: Gila River Arena
mascot: Howler

VANCOUVER CANUCKS
team colors: blue, silver, green and white
home arena: Rogers Arena
mascot: Fin

. . . .

SAN JOSE SHARKS
team colors: teal, black, orange and white
home arena: SAP Center at San Jose
mascot: S.J. Sharkie

CHICAGO BLACKHAWKS
nickname: Hawks
team colors: red, black and white
home arena: United Center
mascot: Tommy Hawk
Stanley Cups won: 6

. . . .

COLORADO AVALANCHE
nickname: Avs
team colors: burgundy, silver, black, blue and white
home arena: Pepsi Center
mascot: Bernie
Stanley Cups won: 2

DALLAS STARS
team colors: green, white, black and silver
home arena: American Airlines Center
Stanley Cups won: 1

. . . .

NASHVILLE PREDATORS
nickname: Preds
team colors: dark blue, white and gold
home arena: Bridgestone Arena
mascot: Gnash

MINNESOTA WILD
team colors: red, green, gold, wheat and white
home arena: Xcel Energy Center
mascot: Nordy

. . . .

WINNIPEG JETS
team colors: dark blue, blue, gray, silver, red and white
home arena: MTS Centre
mascot: Mick E. Moose

. . . .

ST. LOUIS BLUES
team colors: blue, gold, dark blue and white
home arena: Scottrade Center
mascot: Louie

EASTERN CONFERENCE – ATLANTIC DIVISION

TORONTO MAPLE LEAFS
nickname: Leafs
team colors: blue and white
home arena: Air Canada Centre
mascot: Carlton the Bear
Stanley Cups won: 11

. . . .

BUFFALO SABRES
team colors: navy blue, gold, silver and white
home arena: First Niagara Center
mascot: Sabretooth

. . . .

FLORIDA PANTHERS
nickname: Cats
team colors: red, navy blue, yellow, gold and white
home arena: BB&T Center
mascot: Stanley C. Panther

OTTAWA SENATORS
nickname: Sens
team colors: black, red, gold and white
home arena: Canadian Tire Centre
mascot: Spartacat

. . . .

TAMPA BAY LIGHTNING
nickname: Bolts
team colors: blue, black and white
home arena: Amalie Arena
mascot: ThunderBug
Stanley Cups won: 1

MONTREAL CANADIENS
nickname: Habs
team colors: red, blue and white
home arena: Bell Centre
mascot: Youppi
Stanley Cups won: 24

. . . .

DETROIT RED WINGS
nickname: Wings
team colors: red and white
home arena: Joe Louis Arena
mascot (unofficial): Al the Octopus
Stanley Cups won: 11

. . . .

BOSTON BRUINS
nickname: Bs
team colors: gold, black and white
home arena: TD Garden
mascot: Blades the Bruin
Stanley Cups won: 6

EASTERN CONFERENCE – METROPOLITAN DIVISION

NEW YORK RANGERS
nickname: Blueshirts
team colors: blue, white and red
home arena: Madison Square Garden
Stanley Cups won: 4

. . . .

COLUMBUS BLUE JACKETS
nickname: Jackets
team colors: blue, red, silver and white
home arena: Nationwide Arena
mascot: Stinger

. . . .

WASHINGTON CAPITALS
nickname: Caps
team colors: red, navy blue and white
home arena: Verizon Center
mascot: Slapshot

NEW YORK ISLANDERS
nickname: Isles
team colors: orange, blue and white
home arena: Barclays Center
mascot: Sparky the Dragon
Stanley Cups won: 4

. . . .

PITTSBURGH PENGUINS
nickname: Pens
team colors: black, gold and white
home arena: Consol Energy Center
mascot: Iceburgh
Stanley Cups won: 3

PHILADELPHIA FLYERS
team colors: orange, white and black
home arena: Wells Fargo Center
Stanley Cups won: 2

. . . .

NEW JERSEY DEVILS
team colors: red, black and white
home arena: Prudential Center
mascot: N.J. Devil
Stanley Cups won: 3

. . . .

CAROLINA HURRICANES
nickname: Canes
team colors: red, black, gray and white
home arena: PNC Arena
mascot: Stormy
Stanley Cups won: 1

YOUR FAVORITE TEAM

Name of your favorite team: _____

Conference and division: _____

Players on your favorite team at the start of the season:

Number	Name	Position
_____	_____	_____
_____	_____	_____
_____	_____	_____
_____	_____	_____
_____	_____	_____
_____	_____	_____
_____	_____	_____
_____	_____	_____
_____	_____	_____
_____	_____	_____
_____	_____	_____
_____	_____	_____
_____	_____	_____

Changes, Trades, New Players

_____ _____ _____
_____ _____ _____
_____ _____ _____
_____ _____ _____
_____ _____ _____
_____ _____ _____
_____ _____ _____

End-of-Season Standings

Fill in the name of the team you think will finish in first place in each of the four NHL Divisions.

WESTERN CONFERENCE

_____ **PACIFIC DIVISION**

_____ **CENTRAL DIVISION**

EASTERN CONFERENCE

ATLANTIC DIVISION _____

METROPOLITAN DIVISION _____

The Playoffs

Which two teams will meet in the Stanley Cup Final? Fill in their names below, then circle the team you think will win.

Eastern Conference Winner: _____

Western Conference Winner: _____

YOUR FAVORITE TEAM

Your Team — All Season Long

The standings of hockey teams are listed at NHL.com and on the sports pages of the newspaper all season long. The standings will show you which team is in first place, second place, etc., right down to last place.

Some of the abbreviations you'll become familiar with are: GP for games played; W for wins; L for losses; OT for overtime losses; PTS for points; A for assists; G for goals.

Check the standings on the same day of every month and copy down what they say about your team. By keeping track of your team this way you'll be able to see when it was playing well and when it wasn't.

	GP	W	L	OT	PTS
NOVEMBER 1					
DECEMBER 1					
JANUARY 1					
FEBRUARY 1					
MARCH 1					
APRIL 1					
MAY 1					

Final Standings

At the end of the season print the final record of your team below.

YOUR TEAM	GP	W	L	OT	PTS

Your Favorite Players' Scoring Records

While you're keeping track of your favorite team during the season, you can also follow the progress of your favorite players. Just fill in their point totals on the same day of every month.

player	nov 1	dec 1	jan 1	feb 1	mar 1	apr 1	may 1

Your Favorite Goaltenders' Records

You can keep track of your favorite goaltenders' averages during the season. Just fill in the information below.

GAA is the abbreviation for goals-against average. That's the average number of goals given up by a goaltender during a game over the course of the season.

goaltender	nov 1	dec 1	jan 1	feb 1	mar 1	apr 1	may 1

ANAHEIM DUCKS

Denmark isn't known as a country where hockey is hugely popular. According to the International Ice Hockey Federation, there are only about 4,200 registered players in the entire country of 5.5 million people. But hockey was a very popular sport in the house in Herning, Denmark, where Anaheim goalie Frederik Andersen grew up. His father was a goalie on both the local team and Denmark's National Team.

"I was born right into it," recalls Frederik. "Even my mom played, and pretty much every cousin I have. My brothers and sister play too. Pretty much everyone in the family."

"I had the passion for the game. I think you have to love the sport no matter where you are or what country you're from. You gotta love the sport."

Frederik came up through the Danish development system. He played for the local team and also with the National Junior Team. He was impressive enough that he caught the eye of NHL scouts, and he was drafted in 2010 by the Carolina Hurricanes. But Frederik continued to play in Denmark and didn't sign with Carolina. In 2011–2012 he took a big step in the development of his game, leaving the Danish league to go play in the much stronger Swedish Elite League. The move turned out well — he finished with the best goals-against average in the league and was nominated for the league's Rookie of the Year award. His play drew the attention of the Anaheim Ducks, who drafted Frederik in 2012 and quickly signed him to a contract. He worked on his game in the minors with Anaheim's team in Norfolk, Virginia, before stepping into the NHL in 2013–2014.

Last season Frederik finally made his mark in the best league in the world, claiming the job of number-one goalie for the Ducks and finishing among the league leaders with 35 wins. He won 26 of his first 31 decisions — the first NHL goalie ever to do that. With his calm demeanor and another season of NHL experience behind him, the Ducks are confident they have a goalie who can successfully backstop the team as they continue to be a powerhouse in the NHL's Western Conference.

DID YOU KNOW?

Herning, Denmark, where Frederik grew up, is only 56 km (35 miles) from Billund — home of the famous Lego toy company. This is why Frederik's mask has Lego characters on it.

HOCKEY MEMORIES

Frederik played center until he was about 10 years old. He wanted to play goal, but his father always told him no. Finally, one day, he let Frederik strap the pads on.

2014–2015 STATS

GP	W	L	OT	GAA	SO
54	35	12	5	2.38	3

Anaheim Ducks' 3rd choice, 87th overall, in 2012 NHL Entry Draft
1st NHL Team, Season: Anaheim Ducks, 2013–2014
Born: October 2, 1989, in Herning, Denmark
Position: Goaltender
Catches: Left
Height: 1.90 m (6'3")
Weight: 104.5 kg (230 lbs.)

DUSTIN BYFUGLIEN

WINNIPEG JETS

As any Winnipeg fan knows, "Big Buf" can play both forward and defense. He prefers to play back on the blueline and, for most of last season, that's where he was. He started the season playing up front, but on December 5, in a game against the Colorado Avalanche, coach Paul Maurice started Dustin as a defenseman. The switch from forward to the blueline came as a result of a spate of injuries that saw the Jets down to just four regular defensemen. And once Coach Maurice saw how good Dustin looked, the thought of moving him back to forward disappeared. Byfuglien stayed back on defense for most of the rest of the season.

"I knew I'd be back there sooner or later. I just had to complain enough," joked Dustin at the time.

After the switch, Dustin proceeded to go on quite a tear. Over the next 20 games he averaged just under a point per game, scoring six goals and picking up 13 assists. He also led all Winnipeg defensemen in time on the ice, usually playing between 25 and 29 minutes per game. As a result of his great play, Dustin was rewarded with his second career invitation to the NHL All-Star Game. He hadn't been able to play in 2012 because of an injury, so he was excited to be part of the fun this time around.

"He's a horse for that team. I've seen it first-hand when we play them. He can do it all. He's a big piece for their team and he's one of the reasons they are where they are."
— Florida goalie Roberto Luongo on Byfuglien

"It's a great time. There's a great group of guys at the All-Star Game and to be able to sit in the locker room with some of the best guys on the ice right now is an honor. It's really just about enjoying yourself and enjoying being around the guys," said Dustin.

The atmosphere with the Jets was a little more intense as Dustin and his teammates battled to the wire for a playoff spot. Dustin fought through an upper-body injury and played some of the best hockey of his career. The Jets managed to make the playoffs before being eliminated in the first round by Anaheim. However, the entire season was a major step forward for both Dustin and the Jets.

DID YOU KNOW?
When Dustin enjoyed his traditional day with the Cup after being part of the Chicago Blackhawks' championship in 2010, he took it to his hometown of Roseau, Minnesota, where thousands of people lined up to have their photo taken with him and the Stanley Cup.

HOCKEY MEMORIES
When Dustin was a kid, he'd hang out as much as he could with his hockey-playing pals at the Roseau Memorial Arena. His grandmother lived across the road from the rink, so Dustin would drop by for the occasional meal to keep his energy up!

2014–2015 STATS

GP	G	A	PTS
69	18	27	45

Chicago Blackhawks' 8th choice, 245th overall, in 2003 NHL Entry Draft
1st NHL Team, Season: Chicago Blackhawks, 2005–2006
Born: March 27, 1985, in Minneapolis, Minnesota
Position: Defense
Shoots: Right
Height: 1.95 m (6'5")
Weight: 120.5 kg (265 lbs.)

SIDNEY CROSBY

PITTSBURGH PENGUINS

Sidney Crosby, one of the greatest players of his era, is heading into his 11th NHL season as dominant as ever. He finished up last season as the top scorer on the Pittsburgh Penguins, and third in the NHL, with 84 points (28 goals, 56 assists). And while he still has many years to go as a player, it's interesting to look at what he's accomplished in 10 seasons compared to some of the other greats of the game.

It's not really fair to just compare goals, assists and points. Crosby missed the majority of the 2010–2011 and 2011–2012 seasons with post-concussion syndrome. He played only 36 games in 2012–2013 as a result of the NHL lockout. A better comparison is his points-per-game average (the number of points a player has divided by the number of games he has played)

The all-time leader in that category is, unsurprisingly, Wayne Gretzky. Gretzky, the all-time NHL scoring leader, averaged 1.92 points per game during his brilliant career. Gretzky is followed on the list by Mario Lemieux, now Pittsburgh's co-owner and chairman, at 1.88 points per game (regular season).

Next you will find two more Hall of Fame members: Mike Bossy (1.50) and Bobby Orr (1.39). And after that? Sidney Crosby, fifth all-time in points-per-game average with 1.36 points per game at the end of last season. That gives you a pretty good idea of just how great a player he is.

> **"I don't think I've ever had a day where I've stepped back and said: 'I wish I was doing something different.' I'm doing what I love to do."**

"He still has a lot of hockey to play," says former NHL goalie and current TV hockey analyst Darren Pang. "The numbers will tell the tale at the end of his career, but there is no denying even at this stage of his career that he will be considered one of the great players in the history of our game."

When you ask Sid about those kinds of things, you won't get answers as much as just a smile.

"I don't worry about those things. I'm too busy playing the game and just trying to win," says Sid.

DID YOU KNOW?
Sid was offered the captaincy of the Pittsburgh Penguins twice. He turned it down the first time, feeling that, at the time, he was too young for the honor.

HOCKEY MEMORIES
Sidney's early days as an NHLer were made a little easier by living with Pittsburgh co-owner and hockey legend Mario Lemieux and his family. The arrangement worked so well that Sid stayed with them until 2010, when he bought a house in the same area of Pittsburgh.

GP	G	A	PTS
77	28	56	84

Pittsburgh Penguins' 1st choice, 1st overall, in 2005 NHL Entry Draft
1st NHL Team, Season: Pittsburgh Penguins, 2005–2006
Born: August 7, 1987, in Cole Harbour, Nova Scotia
Position: Center
Shoots: Left
Height: 1.80 m (5'11")
Weight: 91 kg (200 lbs.)

JOHNNY GAUDREAU

CALGARY FLAMES

Plenty of people doubted whether Johnny Gaudreau — "Johnny Hockey" to his fans — would ever play in the NHL. Johnny is on the small side for an NHL winger. He is used to doubters; he has heard them all through his hockey life. But his solution is a simple one: ignore them.

"He has been great. He's a real shy, humble little guy," said team captain Mark Giordano last season. "He's pretty quiet and reserved, but a great guy to talk to and definitely a fan favorite in Calgary. He's been amazing."

"The fans are great. I'm really fortunate to get to play in Calgary. They love hockey there and it's really, really great to be part of something special like that."

The Calgary Flames and several other teams were pretty interested in Gaudreau's junior career. Despite his size, he put up numbers larger than most of his opponents' when he played with the Dubuque Fighting Saints in the United States Hockey League during the 2010–2011 season. He scored 36 goals and assisted on 36 more during his rookie season, was named to the USHL All-Rookie Team and was Rookie of the Year. But on NHL Draft Day he was still undrafted as the fourth round started. Tod Button, a Calgary Flames scout, was adamant that the Flames should use their fourth pick to take one of the most exciting players he had ever seen at that level. Jay Feaster, then Calgary's general manager, took his advice and made the pick. Looking back, there definitely wasn't a better fourth-round pick in the draft! There weren't many better picks in the draft, period.

Johnny went on to play three seasons at Boston College after he was drafted. In his final season, he won the Hobey Baker Award as the top player in U.S. college hockey.

Johnny stepped into the Flames lineup last season. By Christmastime he was a fan favorite, and he ended the season as one of three finalists for the Calder Trophy as NHL Rookie of the Year. Even though he didn't win, it was a great accomplishment just to be nominated. As one of Johnny's favorite sayings goes: "Don't believe anyone who says you can't do it."

DID YOU KNOW?

Johnny's first game in the NHL wasn't last season, it was in 2013–2014 when he suited up for the Flames' final regular-season game, against the Vancouver Canucks. He scored his first NHL goal in that game.

HOCKEY MEMORIES

Johnny is grateful for all the love and support he's received from his parents — and one of his happiest memories is of his dad telling him that he was also a small player when he played the game. "All that means is that you have to work harder than everyone else."

GP	G	A	PTS
80	24	40	64

Calgary Flames' 4th choice, 104th overall, in 2011 NHL Entry Draft
1st NHL Team, Season: Calgary Flames, 2014–2015
Born: August 13, 1993, in Salem, New Jersey
Position: Left Wing
Shoots: Left
Height: 1.75 m (5'9")
Weight: 68 kg (150 lbs.)

RYAN GETZLAF

ANAHEIM DUCKS

Although Ryan Getzlaf can definitely score goals, his biggest strength is as a set-up man. He has more than twice as many career assists as goals, and a fair number of those assists have come on goals by his long-time linemate, right-winger Corey Perry. The two were born the same year, drafted the same year (2003) and cracked the Ducks' lineup the same year (2005). They've also played together at two Olympic Games, helping Canada win two Olympic gold medals.

"Me and Corey have developed a great friendship and we work well together," says Ryan. "We've always had the same drive to push one another to be better. We've never been the type to just be content with what we have."

"When I arrived here I knew that I wanted to be a leader with this team at some point. I had to wait my turn, and learn from some guys ahead of me. I feel like it's there now."

There is another thing that the two great linemates share – trust in each other. Trust that one will be where the other expects him to be: for example, if the play is for

a center to drive towards the net, taking a couple of defenders with him, and then drop the puck back to his winger, he has to trust that the winger will be there and he won't end up making a drop pass to an opponent. Effective linemates also trust each other to show up, every night and especially for the big games. Simply put: you have to play hard every night because your linemates' success depends on your efforts. When Ryan is doing things right, that means good things for Perry and vice versa. That's how great linemates work together.

The drive to be better, and showing up to try to be the best, has made Ryan not just a good passer and set-up man, but a great all-around player. He shoots the puck well, he's good on faceoffs, he's a good penalty killer. He has what coaches and players refer to as "the complete package."

"I can't think of many players who have a more complete game than Ryan Getzlaf," says Toronto coach Mike Babcock. "He's tough to defend against because he can do so many things right."

DID YOU KNOW?
Ryan has developed a close friendship with a young man named Hawken Miller, who suffers from a rare form of muscular dystrophy. Hawken is a big Ducks fan, and the two have become friends over the years and draw inspiration from one another.

HOCKEY MEMORIES
One of the great memories for Ryan was being a part of the "Kid Line" with Corey Perry and Dustin Penner during a sensational 2007 playoff run that culminated in the Ducks winning the Stanley Cup.

GP	G	A	PTS
77	25	45	70

Anaheim Ducks' 1st choice, 19th overall, in 2003 NHL Entry Draft
1st NHL Team, Season: Anaheim Ducks, 2005–2006
Born: May 10, 1985, in Regina, Saskatchewan
Position: Center
Shoots: Right
Height: 1.93 m (6'4")
Weight: 100.5 kg (221 lbs.)

TYLER JOHNSON

Second seasons, sometimes called sophomore seasons, can be a mixed bag. Sometimes a rookie can appear on the scene and take opponents by surprise. Then, in the second season, facing high expectations, performance can drop off. Veterans Jeff Carter and Jordan Staal are both examples of players whose sophomore seasons were disappointing compared to their rookie years.

Tyler Johnson had the opposite kind of sophomore season. He finished 2013–2014 tied for first in rookie goal scoring and was nominated for the Calder Trophy as Rookie of the Year. Expectations were high for his second season, and he met them all, performing even better than he had as a rookie. Tyler led the Lightning in scoring for much of last season and ended up tied with Steven Stamkos for the team scoring lead. He then led the team in playoff scoring with 23 points (13 goals, 10 assists) during the Bolts' march to the Stanley Cup final.

"A lot of it is confidence," says Tyler. "You come into the NHL and you just don't want to make mistakes and be the guy who costs the team a goal. Now it's more about making the play. Playing that way got me to the NHL, and with time, good coaching and playing with good players, it starts to happen."

> "I think you have to have part of that 'kid mentality' where you want to come to the rink every day and want to improve and just have fun doing it."

"I see determination from the guy," says veteran Braydon Coburn, who joined Tampa last season at the trade deadline. "This guy is smart. He knows how to play the game. He's a small guy, but I don't think he views himself as small."

There many things about Tyler's play that are impressive. One of the compliments you hear most often is that he has a good "hockey IQ." That's a way of saying that Tyler doesn't just play the game, he also understands the game.

A good rookie season followed by a very good second season means that season number three probably can't start soon enough for Tyler Johnson.

DID YOU KNOW?

As a six-year-old, Tyler played in one of the mini-games held during intermissions at the games of the local junior team, the Spokane Chiefs. Nine years later he was drafted by the Chiefs and a couple of years after that, he was playing for them.

HOCKEY MEMORIES

Tyler still remembers the long car rides with his parents to go from his home in Spokane, Washington, up to Vancouver to play hockey. "Seven hours in the back of a van just to go play hockey. Now I'm going to the games on planes. It's pretty special the way things have turned out."

2014–2015 STATS

GP	G	A	PTS
77	29	43	72

Not drafted — signed as a free agent by Tampa Bay, March 7, 2011
1st NHL Team, Season: Tampa Bay Lightning, 2013–2014
Born: July 29, 1990. in Spokane, Washington
Position: Center
Shoots: Right
Height: 1.73 m (5'8")
Weight: 82.5 kg (182 lbs.)

At age 25, Erik Karlsson heads into this season as winner of the Norris Trophy for the NHL's best defenseman. Expectations will be high for the young player, as they were the year before, when Erik was named the ninth captain in the history of the franchise. His mentor, Daniel Alfredsson, had worn the "C" with pride from 1999 to 2013. Alfredsson was followed as captain by Jason Spezza —another veteran from the same era. But Spezza was traded to the Dallas Stars in the off-season and that meant that the Senators needed to name a new captain. The choice was an obvious one, and the torch was passed from one generation of Ottawa Senators stars to the next. Erik was poised to be the next great Ottawa Senators player and leader.

"I will never be Alfie. I will never be Spezza. I have to be myself," said Erik at the time. "I will lead in a different way than other players will. That's how it is for everyone."

Alfredsson, who left the Senators for Detroit in a contract dispute and then officially retired at the start of last season because of back problems, was a close friend to Erik when the two were together in Ottawa. Erik lived with Alfredsson and his family when he arrived in Ottawa as a 19-year-old. He learned a lot about leadership by watching how Alfredsson did it.

"He didn't have to say a lot at times. He always decided to do things by action rather than by talking about it," says Erik.

Last season, Erik and the Senators went on one of the greatest late-season sprints for a playoff spot that the NHL has seen in recent times. Two major factors were the goaltending of Andrew "The Hamburglar" Hammond and the play of Erik.

> "I want to be that kind of player. I want to have responsibility. I want to be a big part of everything we have going on."

The Senators, against all odds, made the playoffs and faced the Montreal Canadiens in the first round. Although they fell to Montreal in six hard-fought games, the Sens and their fans have reason to expect even more from their team, and their captain, this season.

DID YOU KNOW?

Erik loves to play golf. He doesn't consider himself to be a great golfer, but he enjoys time on the course with his friends. He counts PGA Tour pro and Ottawa native Brad Fritsch among his friends.

HOCKEY MEMORIES

One of Erik's earliest hockey memories is of wanting to be a goalie. His dad took a slapshot at him when he was in goal and Erik remembers that he started crying. That was it for his goaltending career!

2014–2015 STATS

GP	G	A	PTS
82	21	45	66

Ottawa Senators' 1st choice, 15th overall, in 2008 NHL Entry Draft
1st NHL Team, Season: Ottawa Senators, 2009–2010
Born: May 31, 1990, in Landsbro, Sweden
Position: Defense
Shoots: Right
Height: 1.83 m (6')
Weight: 82 kg (180 lbs.)

Over the 10 seasons since Alex Ovechkin first stepped onto the ice in the NHL, no other player in the game has scored more goals (475), recorded more points (895), had more multi-goal games (100) or scored more game-winning goals (80). And Alex does it all with an enthusiasm that is fun to watch. He pumps his arm or jumps up against the glass to celebrate a big goal. He will deal out a big bodycheck, but he will also take a big bodycheck and jump back to his skates, chirping at his opponent as if to say: "I'm fine, you can't stop me."

Last season was a bit of a reset for the Washington Capitals. There was a new coach, Barry Trotz, and a new general manager, Brian MacLellan. Some wondered how Ovie would adjust to a new coach with different methods. As it turned out, there was no need to worry. One adjustment Trotz made was to play Ovie more on the left wing than the right wing. Trotz had watched highlights of Ovechkin goals from the previous season and noticed that, despite playing right wing, he scored most of his goals from the left side of the ice. This seemed to show that Ovie was more comfortable on the left than the right.

Ovie's magic was there once again last season. He picked up the sixth 50-goal season of his career and his highest point total since 2010–2011. However, hockey's biggest prize is still the one that Alex hasn't been able to add to his trophy case. Ovie and the Caps were frustrated again last season as they bowed out in overtime in the seventh, and deciding, game of their second-round series against the New York Rangers.

"He plays every game like it's his last game. That's what I love about watching him."
— Hall of Famer Wayne Gretzky talking about Alex Ovechkin

"Stanley Cup is the biggest prize. It's the one I want the most," says Ovie.

DID YOU KNOW?

Alex is the only player in NHL history to be named to the First All-Star Team in each of the first five seasons of his career. He has been named a First Team All Star seven times in his career so far.

HOCKEY MEMORIES

Alex's father remembers two-year-old Alex telling him "No, no," if he turned the TV off when there was a hockey game on. "He cried until the hockey was back on," recalls his father with a smile.

2014–2015 STATS

GP	G	A	PTS
81	53	28	81

Washington Capitals' 1st choice, 1st overall, in 2004 NHL Entry Draft
1st NHL Team, Season: Washington Capitals, 2005–2006
Born: September 17, 1985, in Moscow, USSR (now Russia)
Position: Left Wing
Shoots: Right
Height: 1.90 m (6'3")
Weight: 104.5 kg (230 lbs.)

CAREY PRICE

To use a phrase from another sport, Montreal's Carey Price belted it out of the park last season. He was the backbone of the Montreal Canadiens all season long. Along the way he picked up the William Jennings Trophy for the team with the lowest goals-against average, the Vezina Trophy as the NHL's top goalie, the Ted Lindsay Award as the most outstanding player as selected by NHL players and, the biggest individual prize, the Hart Trophy as the NHL's Most Valuable Player.

Carey's stellar play last season was just a continuation of his play in 2013–2014, when he helped Canada win a gold medal at the 2014 Sochi Olympics and then led Montreal to a seven-game victory over the Boston Bruins in the second round of the playoffs. To the amazement of his opponents, Carey continues to find ways to get better.

> "Personally, I think a shutout is a team stat; it's not an individual stat. We've been committed to playing team defense all year and that number reflects that."

"I don't know if it's just maturity or just knowing that you have the ability or whatever it is, you just go out and do your job," Carey told reporters last year. "Of course you need a team in front of you to play well. I am at a stage where I totally trust the guys that are playing around me and that's the truth. All I worry about is making that first save, and then I know the guys will be there. When you can do that, it really simplifies things."

As last season went on and the games became more and more important, Carey's game got better and better. During February, March and April, his record was an amazing 16-6-4 with a 1.88 goals against average. He also had 5 shutouts during that same stretch. One of the funniest quotes of the year came after another great performance from Carey when his coach, Michel Therrien, remarked that "Price was even Pricier than he usually is."

Throughout his career Carey has displayed an amazing ability to adapt his game, to continue to develop and to rise to the occasion. There is no reason to doubt that he will do the same this season. He is one of the greats of his era.

DID YOU KNOW?

Last season Carey became only the third goalie in NHL history to play a minimum of 50 regular-season games and finish with a save percentage of .933 or higher (the other two are Dominik Hasek and Tim Thomas).

HOCKEY MEMORIES

To win a gold medal playing for your country at the Olympic Games, as Carey did for Canada in Sochi, is something truly memorable. To also be named as the top goaltender at the tournament, as Carey was, makes the memory even more precious.

GP	W	L	OT	GAA	SO
66	44	16	6	1.96	9

Montreal Canadiens' 1st choice, 5th overall, in 2005 NHL Entry Draft
1st NHL Team, Season: Montreal Canadiens, 2007–2008
Born: August 16, 1987 in Anahim Lake, British Columbia
Position: Goaltender
Catches: Left
Height: 1.90 m (6'3")
Weight: 96.5 kg (212 lbs.)

HENRIK SEDIN

Henrik Sedin scored his first NHL point during a game against the Florida Panthers on October 6, 2000. It was an assist. More than 14 years and 1,073 games later, Henrik notched the 900th point of his career. That milestone came in a game against the San Jose Sharks on March 3, 2015. The point, a goal, was like so many of the goals that the Swedish superstar has scored during his great career in Vancouver: the puck was fired towards the goal and was loose in front. His brother Daniel battled for possession and tipped it back to the right wing faceoff circle where Henrik pounced on it and drilled it home for the goal.

Henrik and his twin brother, Daniel, have shared several different linemates over the years, but the two have always played together and, in the words of Henrik: "It's sometimes like we have one brain.

"Off the ice it's maybe not like that. But, on the ice, I don't think it's because we're twins, but because we've played so long together. I think if you put me on a line with anyone else and we played on the same line for 20 years, we're going to think hockey the same way."

Last season was a bounce-back season of sorts for both Henrik and the Canucks. The team finished in second place in the Pacific Division after missing the playoffs the season before, although they suffered a disappointing first-round exit. And Henrik rebounded from a disappointing 2013–2014, when he battled injuries and finished with only 50 points in 70 games. Last season Henrik was healthy and picked up a much improved 73 points (18 goals, 55 assists).

"Being so close a few years back [the Canucks lost in the seventh game of the 2011 Stanley Cup Final], that's something that comes up a lot. We have one more thing to win, and that's our only goal."

"There were lots of changes, a lot of good changes, I feel," said Henrik. "We lost some good players, but we also got some young, up-and-coming players."

The hope for Canucks fans is that Henrik, along with those younger players, will continue to make Vancouver one of the best in the west.

DID YOU KNOW?

Henrik is only the fourth Swedish-born NHL player to hit the 900-career-point mark. The other three (Mats Sundin, Daniel Alfredsson and Nicklas Lidstrom) all went on to score over a thousand career points.

HOCKEY MEMORIES

Henrik started playing hockey at a very young age. He remembers that both he and his brother Daniel played center. They didn't start playing on the same line regularly until several years later, when they were 14 and Daniel switched from center to wing.

2014–2015 STATS

GP	G	A	PTS
82	18	55	73

Vancouver Canucks' 2nd choice, 3rd overall, in 1999 NHL Entry Draft
1st NHL Team, Season: Vancouver Canucks, 2000–2001
Born: September 26, 1980, in Ornskoldsvik, Sweden
Position: Center
Shoots: Left
Height: 1.88 m (6'2")
Weight: 85.5 kg (188 lbs.)

TYLER SEGUIN

DALLAS STARS

A hockey career is something that develops at a different pace and in different ways for every player. Some players, like Alex Ovechkin, seem to adapt almost immediately to what it takes to play in the NHL. Some players take a few seasons for their game to reach the high level people expect of superstars. For Dallas center Tyler Seguin it took a few seasons, as well as a change of scenery, for him to hit the heights of offensive greatness. Last season was Tyler's fifth NHL season and the best of his career so far. He finished second in team scoring and seventh in the NHL with 77 points (37 goals, 40 assists).

> **"I want to be the best I can be no matter what the circumstances. That's how I was raised."**

Tyler was drafted by the Boston Bruins in 2010, second overall. He had a decent, although not outstanding, rookie season. The highlight for him was being part of a Stanley Cup Championship with the Bruins in that first season. He went on to play in his second Cup Final with Boston two seasons later. That time his play didn't meet expectations, as the Bruins lost to Chicago in the final in six games. Tyler had only eight points in 22 playoff games. His play and his work ethic were criticized by Peter Chiarelli, then Boston general manager, and a few weeks after the season was over Tyler was dealt to Dallas.

"Like anybody, I had to mature," says Tyler. "Getting traded was something that opened my eyes a little. I came here [Dallas] and they told me that they wanted me to be a leader. I took that seriously and wanted to be what they wanted me to be. It's all a learning process, especially when you're eighteen and coming into the league. I feel now like I've adapted to my surroundings and being a professional."

An added bonus of moving to Dallas was that Tyler was able to move to his natural center position, rather than playing out of position on the right wing as he had been in Boston. He has worked brilliantly on a line with veteran Jamie Benn.

"We make one another better," says Tyler. "It's all good."

DID YOU KNOW?

Tyler has a full sleeve of tattoos on each arm. On the left, he has the birth years of both of his parents and his two sisters, as well as an angel, a family tree and a heart.

HOCKEY MEMORIES

Winning the Stanley Cup, in his rookie season, is a memory that Tyler thinks won't be topped until he's able to win another, in a Dallas sweater.

GP	G	A	PTS
71	37	40	77

Boston Bruins' 1st choice, 2nd overall, in 2010 NHL Entry Draft
1st NHL Team, Season: Boston Bruins, 2010–2011
Born: January 31, 1992, in Brampton, Ontario
Position: Center
Shoots: Right
Height: 1.85 m (6'1")
Weight: 88.5 kg (195 lbs.)

It was a long way back from one year earlier, but it was great to see a smile on the face of Tampa Bay Lightning superstar Steve Stamkos late last season.

"Its been a lot of fun to be able to play, to come back and to just feel good again. That's been the exciting thing for me this season," Steve told a group of reporters late last season.

Back on November 11, 2013, it was quite a different story. About midway through the second period of a game against the Boston Bruins, Steve bumped with a Boston defenseman and lost his balance. He slid into the goalpost, and his right leg took the impact. The end result was a broken shin bone. He made it back for the final part of the 2013–2014 season, but his dream of playing for Canada at the 2014 Sochi Olympics was crushed. It was a tough pill to swallow for Steve. Even at training camp last season, he was still aware of the injury.

"I want to get to the point where I wake up in the morning and don't even realize that the injury had happened," said Steve.

He felt as though he had reached that point, or very close to it, by the stretch run last season. He finished up the season with 72 points (43 goals, 29 assists) — not quite at his career-high level of 60 goals and 97 points, in 2011–2012, but still impressive enough to finish tied for tops on his team and 14th in the league. Steve also helped to pace the team in the playoffs with 18 points (7 goals, 11 assists) as the Lightning battled their way to the Stanley Cup Final.

"As a player you want to be on a good team, and we have a good team. We have a good thing going. We want to be consistently in the mix."

But Steve is much more than just a goal scorer for Tampa. He's the captain and one of the leaders of the team.

"Off the ice he's a great guy. He cares about the team," says teammate Jonathan Drouin. "He's our captain for a reason. He leads on and off the ice."

DID YOU KNOW?

Steve's dad was a huge fan of the Toronto Maple Leafs. He took a ticket stub from the game the Leafs played on February 7, 1990, the day Steve was born, and had it made into a medallion.

HOCKEY MEMORIES

Steve was on the Canadian National Junior Team that won the 2008 World Junior Championship in overtime against Sweden. "All I remember is seeing the ref pointing to the net and signaling the goal and all of us that were on the bench just jumped."

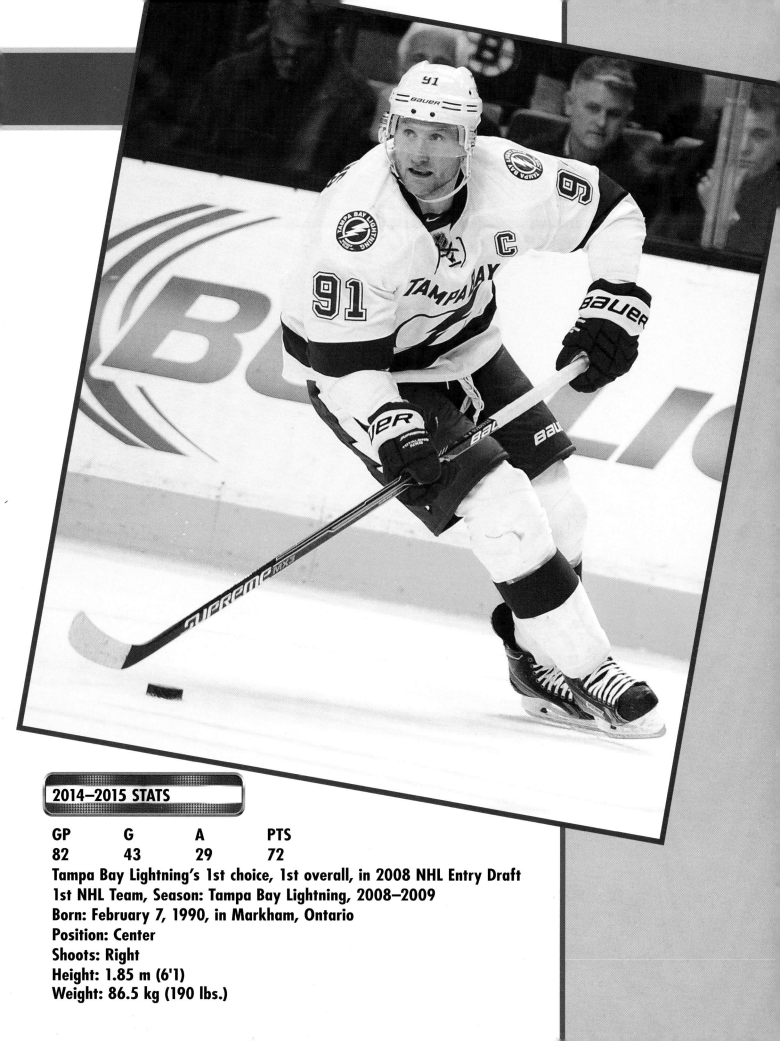

2014–2015 STATS

GP	G	A	PTS
82	43	29	72

Tampa Bay Lightning's 1st choice, 1st overall, in 2008 NHL Entry Draft
1st NHL Team, Season: Tampa Bay Lightning, 2008–2009
Born: February 7, 1990, in Markham, Ontario
Position: Center
Shoots: Right
Height: 1.85 m (6'1)
Weight: 86.5 kg (190 lbs.)

P.K. SUBBAN

P.K. Subban is one of the biggest stars in the game, and he has a personality as big as his talent. Unlike many big stars, P.K. loves to show his emotion on the ice. He gets excited when he makes a big hit, he raises his arms and smiles when he scores, and he loves to "chirp" opponents to see if he can get them off their game. He looks and acts like he's enjoying himself out there. That approach can be fine, but you have to be able to back it up with terrific play, and that's exactly what P.K. does. Last season he was, for the fifth season in a row, the top-scoring defenseman on the Habs. He plays more than any other player on the team, an average of 30 shifts, with an average ice time of over 26 minutes per game. P.K. also won the Norris Trophy as the NHL's top defenseman in 2012–2013 and was one of the contenders for the award last season.

"I think he's a special guy on and off the ice," said young Montreal defenseman Nathan Beaulieu last season. "It's hard not to admire his passion for the game and the way it can influence people."

One of Subban's biggest strengths is his skating ability. He owes some of that to his father who, as an 11-year-old immigrant to Canada, used to watch and admire the skills of the players in this new game in his new country. P.K.'s father knew how important skating was to the success of any hockey player, and he made an effort to try to skate with his son every day, all winter. Some days, when Subban's father had to work late, he'd wake P.K. up when he got home and take him out for a late-night skate before sending him back to bed.

"Those are memories that still put a smile on my face," says P.K.

"I always wanted to be a good hockey player. I wanted to be like the guys in TV. It wasn't until I was 9 or 10, when I realized I was one of the best players in my age group, that I started to develop a hunger to make the NHL."

A player with a big personality will always have his critics, as well as admirers. P.K. tries to downplay both sides. He just wants to go out there, have fun, be the best and win. He's doing quite well on all three counts.

DID YOU KNOW?

As good as P.K. is, he's been quoted as saying that his youngest brother, Vancouver Canucks draft pick Jordan Subban, will be "the best of all of us."

HOCKEY MEMORIES

There is a story that, as a kid, P.K. fired a slapshot that was so hard it cracked the mask of the goalie whose head got in front of it. After the game the other player quit as a goalie, deciding that maybe forward or defense would be a little more fun.

2014–2015 STATS

GP	G	A	PTS
82	15	45	60

Montreal Canadiens' 3rd choice, 43rd overall, in 2007 NHL Entry Draft
1st NHL Team, Season: Montreal Canadiens, 2010–2011
Born: May 13, 1989, in Toronto, Ontario
Position: Defense
Shoots: Right
Height: 1.83 m (6')
Weight: 98.5 kg (217 lbs.)

NEW YORK ISLANDERS

If you're a hockey fan, and particularly if you're a New York Islanders fan, you have to smile when you think about how much better John Tavares will get. John is an elite player now, but he's only 25 years old and just heading into the prime of his NHL career. He's already stacked up 401 career points and in the last couple of seasons has emerged as the offensive heart of the Islanders. As he's become better, the team around him has improved as well. The Islanders have gone from a team that finished 26th out of 30 teams in his rookie season (2009–2010) and didn't score a lot of goals to a team that had the tenth-best record in the league and the fourth-best offence.

> **"Whether it's shooting the puck or distributing it, he sees the puck at a different level than almost any other player I've ever seen."**
> — **Islanders general manager Garth Snow**

"I think you always have confidence that things will improve," says Tavares. "I think I always believe in myself and believe in the work you put into your game, and the things you do to prepare."

In Tavares' five full NHL seasons (not counting the lockout-shortened 2012–2013 season) he has topped the 60-point mark four times. He has also matured and become one of the leaders on the team. However, John is quick to note that the Islanders' improvement comes down to more factors than just his ability to score points. He points to some key trades and the great work by the coaching staff and head coach Jack Capuano.

"They [the coaching staff] really challenged us into the summer and training camp about the way we wanted to approach things. They had high expectations of us and really pushed us in that direction."

John is coming into the prime years of his career, and his work ethic and approach to every game are second to none.

"Every game I make sure I try to do everything I can to feel as best I can and feel as prepared as I can be. There are no excuses when you play at this level."

Those are great points, from the man who scores a lot of points.

DID YOU KNOW?

John's number 91 was retired by his junior hockey team, the Oshawa Generals. He's only the fourth player in Generals history to have his number retired. John had a franchise record 183 goals in 223 games.

HOCKEY MEMORIES

John recalls being totally focused on hockey as a kid. His first crayon drawings were of hockey players and he built hockey sticks out of Lego. "The desire has never stopped. It has only grown. My passion has been there since day one."

2014–2015 STATS

GP	G	A	PTS
82	38	48	86

New York Islanders' 1st choice, 1st overall, in 2009 NHL Entry Draft
1st NHL Team, Season: New York Islanders, 2009–2010
Born: September 20, 1990, in Mississauga, Ontario
Position: Center
Shoots: Left
Height: 1.85 m (6'1")
Weight: 93 kg (205 lbs.)

JAKUB VORACEK

To hear Jakub Voracek talk, nobody was more surprised that he was the NHL's leading scorer at the All-Star break than Jakub himself (he ended up finishing fifth in league scoring with 81 points).

"I have to say, it's only the All-Star break," he joked. "The guys who are on top, they do it for ten years. I'm happy with how I'm playing, but I'm not getting carried away.

"I don't know whether it was experience or great teammates or playing on a good power play. I do know that I always say that 'the team makes the player.' If you have a good team, a good bunch of guys, you always feel better on the ice," Jakub said.

More specifically, in Jake's case, it's his linemate who has helped make the player. There is no doubt that the Flyers have been a great fit for Voracek since he was traded to them from Columbus, but playing on the same line as Claude Giroux for the last three seasons has really helped his game and point totals.

"I think they're both pretty good at everything," says veteran teammate Vincent Lecavalier. "Claude is a smart player and passes the puck at just the right time, and Jake has good speed and takes the puck to the net. It works well together."

> "He's shooting pucks, getting to the net, things like that. A guy with that skill, and he does the right things all the time, he's going to produce."
> — Philadelphia coach Craig Berube

Jake's breakout season wasn't a complete surprise. When you look back over the previous few seasons, you can see that he was improving. He finished up with 46 points (22 goals, 24 assists) during the shortened 2012–2013 season, averaging almost a point per game. He followed that up with a career high 62 points (23 goals, 39 assists) in 2013–2014, despite being hurt at the start of that season.

Last season, Jake's seventh in the NHL, it all came together for him, as he had his best season ever.

The better you get in the NHL, the tougher it is to continue to improve. It's the best league in the world. Opponents adjust; good players do the same. That's the next challenge for Jake.

DID YOU KNOW?
Jakub made a decision heading into last season that he would shoot the puck more. He ended up taking more shots on goal than he had any other season.

HOCKEY MEMORIES
Jakub was on the Czech team that won the World Hockey Championship in 2010. "No one expected us to win, but sometimes you get some luck," recalls Jake.

2014–2015 STATS

GP	G	A	PTS
82	22	59	81

Columbus Blue Jackets' 1st choice, 7th overall, in 2007 NHL Entry Draft
1st NHL Team, Season: Columbus Blue Jackets, 2008–2009
Born: August 15, 1989, in Kladno, Czechoslovakia (now Czech Republic)
Position: Right Wing
Shoots: Left
Height: 1.88 m (6'2")
Weight: 97 kg (214 lbs.)

SHEA WEBER

NASHVILLE PREDATORS

There are many aspects to Shea Weber's game that help make him one of the top defensemen in the world. To start with, he plays a lot and during most of the key situations for his team — power plays and penalty killing. Shea's average ice time during a game is about 26 and a half minutes; that's one of the highest per-game totals in the NHL. Shea doesn't back down from tough play, either. He's one of the top-hitting defensemen on his team, finishing last season with 166 hits. And he is a leader. He's been the captain of the Nashville Predators, the only NHL team he's ever played for, since the 2010–2011 season.

"When you have team success, individual success kind of comes with it."

"You tell me who is making more of a contribution to their team than Shea Weber has made to the Nashville Predators both on and off the ice," says Nashville general manager David Poile.

The thing that most people talk about when the subject of Shea

Weber comes up is his awesomely powerful slapshot. It is the hardest in the NHL. Last season, during the NHL Skills Competition, Shea's shot was measured at 108.5 mph (174.4 km/h). That works out to about 159 feet (48.5 meters) per second. The distance from the blueline to the goal crease on an NHL rink is 64 feet (19.5 meters), so if Shea blasts a slapshot from just inside the blueline, the goalie will have approximately .39 seconds to react — literally the blink of an eye! It's only a hair short of the fastest shot ever timed, by Boston veteran defenseman Zdeno Chara back in 2012. His shot was clocked at 108.8 mph. (175.1 km/h).

"Chara is the guy to beat all the time," says Shea. "But I just want to keep getting better every year. As kids we strive to get better at everything we do and it's no different now."

Shea finished up last season with 45 points (15 goals, 30 assists) and, as he heads into his 11th season with the Preds, many feel his best years are still to come.

DID YOU KNOW?

When he was young, Shea worked on his shot in the driveway after school. He'd put a piece of plywood his Dad had brought home from work onto the driveway. Then he'd put pucks onto the smooth, ice-like surface of the wood and shoot at tin can targets to improve his shot.

HOCKEY MEMORIES

Shea has played for Team Canada many times in his career: a World Junior Championship, two World Championships and two Olympic Games. He says: "You grow up watching guys play for their country and it never gets tired. It's always a thrill."

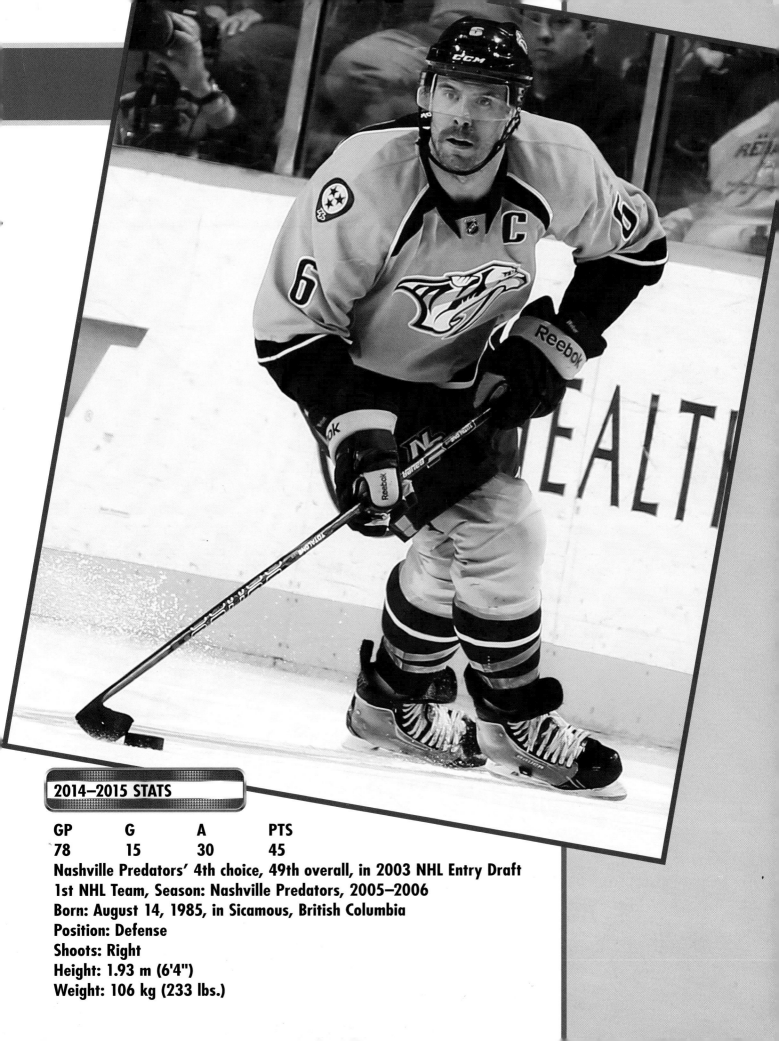

2014–2015 STATS

GP	G	A	PTS
78	15	30	45

Nashville Predators' 4th choice, 49th overall, in 2003 NHL Entry Draft
1st NHL Team, Season: Nashville Predators, 2005–2006
Born: August 14, 1985, in Sicamous, British Columbia
Position: Defense
Shoots: Right
Height: 1.93 m (6'4")
Weight: 106 kg (233 lbs.)

REFEREE SIGNALS

Do you know what is happening when the referee stops play and makes a penalty call? If you don't, then you're missing an important part of the game. The referee can call different penalties that result in anything from playing a man short for two minutes to having a player kicked out of the game.

Here are some of the most common referee signals. Now you'll know what penalties are being called against your team.

Boarding
Checking an opponent into the boards in a violent way.

Charging
Checking an opponent in a violent way as a result of skating or charging at him.

Cross-checking
Striking an opponent with the stick, while both hands are on the stick and both arms are extended.

Elbowing
Checking an opponent with an elbow.

High-sticking
Striking an opponent with the stick, which is held above shoulder height.

Holding
Holding back an opponent with the hands or arms.

Hooking
Using the blade of the stick to hold back an opponent.

Icing
Shooting the puck across the opposing team's goal line from one's own side of the rink. Called only if the opposing player touches the puck first.

Interference
Holding back an opponent who does not have the puck in play.

Kneeing
Using a knee to hold back an opponent.

Misconduct
A ten-minute penalty — the longest type called. Usually for abuse of an official.

Roughing
Shoving or striking an opponent.

REFEREE SIGNALS

Slashing
Using the stick to strike an opponent.

Spearing
Poking an opponent with the blade of the stick.

Slow whistle
The official waits to blow his whistle because of a delayed offside or delayed penalty call. Done while the opposing team has control of the puck.

Tripping
Tripping an opponent with the stick, a hand or a foot.

Unsportsmanlike conduct
Showing poor sportsmanship toward an opponent. For example: biting, pulling hair, etc.

Wash-out
Goal not allowed.

FINAL TEAM STANDINGS 2014–2015

EASTERN CONFERENCE

Atlantic Division

Team	GP	W	L	OT	PTS
MONTREAL	82	50	22	10	110
TAMPA BAY	82	50	24	8	108
DETROIT	82	43	25	14	100
OTTAWA	82	43	26	13	99
BOSTON	82	41	27	14	96
FLORIDA	82	38	29	15	91
TORONTO	82	30	44	8	68
BUFFALO	82	23	51	8	54

Metropolitan Division

Team	GP	W	L	OT	PTS
NY RANGERS	82	53	22	7	113
WASHINGTON	82	45	26	11	101
NY ISLANDERS	82	47	28	7	101
PITTSBURGH	82	43	27	12	98
COLUMBUS	82	42	35	5	89
PHILADELPHIA	82	33	31	18	84
NEW JERSEY	82	32	36	14	78
CAROLINA	82	30	41	11	71

WESTERN CONFERENCE

Pacific Division

Team	GP	W	L	OT	PTS
ANAHEIM	82	51	24	7	109
VANCOUVER	82	48	29	5	101
CALGARY	82	45	30	7	97
LOS ANGELES	82	40	27	15	95
SAN JOSE	82	40	33	9	89
EDMONTON	82	24	44	14	62
ARIZONA	82	24	50	8	56

Central Division

Team	GP	W	L	OT	PTS
ST. LOUIS	82	51	24	7	109
NASHVILLE	82	47	25	10	104
CHICAGO	82	48	28	6	102
MINNESOTA	82	46	28	8	100
WINNIPEG	82	43	26	13	99
DALLAS	82	41	31	10	92
COLORADO	82	39	31	12	90

GP = Games played; W = Wins; L = Losses; OT = Overtime; PTS = Points

Top Ten Points Leaders 2014–2015

	PLAYER	TEAM	GP	G	A	P	S	S%
1	JAMIE BEAN	DALLAS	82	35	52	87	253	13.8
2	JOHN TAVARES	NY ISLANDERS	82	38	48	86	278	13.7
3	SIDNEY CROSBY	PITTSBURGH	77	28	56	84	237	11.8
4	ALEX OVECHKIN	WASHINGTON	81	53	28	81	395	13.4
5	JAKUB VORACEK	PHILADELPHIA	82	22	59	81	221	10.0
6	NICKLAS BACKSTROM	WASHINGTON	82	18	60	78	153	11.8
7	TYLER SEGUIN	DALLAS	71	37	40	77	280	13.2
8	JIRI HUDLER	CALGARY	78	31	45	76	158	19.6
9	DANIEL SEDIN	VANCOUVER	82	20	56	76	226	8.8
10	VLADIMIR TARASENKO	ST. LOUIS	77	37	36	73	264	14.0

GP = Games played; G = Goals; A = Assists; P = Points;
S = Shots; S% = Percentage

Top Ten Goalies — Total Wins 2014–2015

	PLAYER	TEAM	GP	W	L	OT	SA%	GA	GAA
1	CAREY PRICE	MONTREAL	66	44	16	6	0.933	130	1.96
2	PEKKA RINNE	NASHVILLE	64	41	17	6	0.923	140	2.18
3	BRADEN HOLTBY	WASHINGTON	73	41	20	10	0.923	157	2.22
4	BEN BISHOP	TAMPA BAY	62	40	13	5	0.916	136	2.32
5	JAROSLAV HALAK	NY ISLANDERS	59	38	17	4	0.914	144	2.43
6	DEVAN DUBNYK	ARIZONA MINNESOTA	58	36	14	4	0.929	115	2.07
7	JONATHAN QUICK	LOS ANGELES	72	36	22	13	0.918	156	2.24
8	FREDERIK ANDERSEN	ANAHEIM	54	35	12	5	0.914	123	2.38
9	TUUKKA RASK	BOSTON	70	34	21	13	0.922	156	2.3
10	MARC-ANDRE FLEURY	PITTSBURGH	64	34	20	9	0.92	146	2.32

GP = Games played; W = Wins; L = Losses; OT = Overtime and/or Shut-Out Losses;
SA% = Save percentage; GA = Goals Against; GAA = Goals-Against Average

END-OF-SEASON STATS

Countdown to the Cup 2015–2016

EASTERN CONFERENCE

STANLEY CUP
FINAL

CONFERENCE
FINAL

ROUND
TWO

ROUND
ONE

THE CHAMPION:

WESTERN CONFERENCE

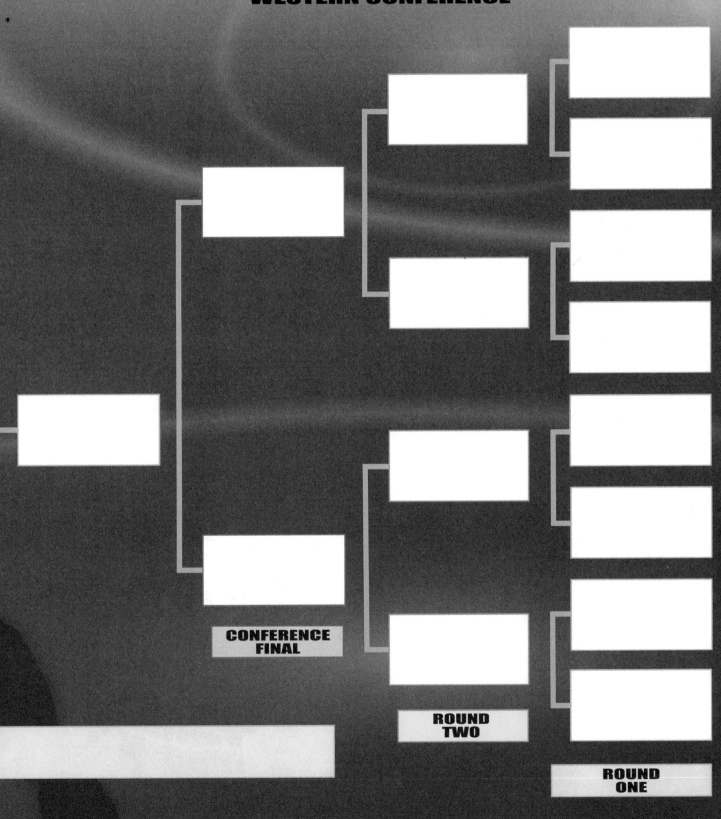

CONFERENCE
FINAL

ROUND
TWO

ROUND
ONE

NHL AWARDS

Here are some of the major NHL awards for individual players. Fill in your selection for each award and then fill in the name of the actual winner of the trophy.

HART MEMORIAL TROPHY

Awarded to the player judged to be the most valuable to his team. Selected by the Professional Hockey Writers Association.

2015 winner: **Carey Price**

Your choice for 2016: _____

The winner: _____

ART ROSS TROPHY

Awarded to the player who leads the league in scoring points at the end of the regular season.

2015 winner: **Jamie Benn**

Your choice for 2016: _____

The winner: _____

CALDER MEMORIAL TROPHY

Awarded to the player selected as the most proficient in his first year of competition in the NHL. Selected by the Professional Hockey Writers Association.

2015 winner: **Aaron Ekblad**

Your choice for 2016: _____

The winner: _____

JAMES NORRIS TROPHY

Awarded to the defense player who demonstrates throughout his season the greatest all-round ability. Selected by the Professional Hockey Writers Association.

2015 winner: **Erik Karlsson**

Your choice for 2016: _____

The winner: _____

VEZINA TROPHY

Awarded to the goalkeeper judged to be the best. Selected by the NHL general managers.

2015 winner: **Carey Price**

Your choice for 2016: _____

The winner: _____

MAURICE RICHARD TROPHY

Awarded to the player who scores the highest number of regular-season goals.

2015 winner: **Alex Ovechkin**

Your choice for 2016: _____

The winner: _____

FRANK J. SELKE TROPHY

Awarded to the forward who best excels in the defensive aspects of the game. Selected by the Professional Hockey Writers Association.

2015 winner: **Patrice Bergeron**

Your choice for 2016: _____

The winner: _____

WILLIAM M. JENNINGS TROPHY

Awarded to the goalkeeper(s) who played a minimum of 25 games for the team with the fewest goals scored against it.

2015 winners: **Corey Crawford and Carey Price**

Your choice for 2016: _____

The winner: _____

CONN SMYTHE TROPHY

Awarded to the player most valuable to his team in the Stanley Cup playoffs. Selected by the Professional Hockey Writers Association.

2015 winner: **Duncan Keith**

Your choice for 2016: _____

The winner: _____

LADY BYNG MEMORIAL TROPHY

Awarded to the player judged to have exhibited the best sportsmanship combined with a high standard of playing ability. Selected by the Professional Hockey Writers Association.

2015 winner: **Jiri Hudler**

Your choice for 2016: _____

The winner: _____

BILL MASTERTON MEMORIAL TROPHY

Awarded to the player who best exemplifies the qualitites of perseverance, sportsmanship and dedication to hockey. Selected by the Professional Hockey Writers Association.

2015 winner: **Devan Dubnyk**

Your choice for 2016: _____

The winner: _____

AUTHOR'S ACKNOWLEDGEMENTS: Thanks to NHL.com, NHLPA.com, the Hockey Hall of Fame, and the personal websites of players profiled as well as IIHF.com, hockeydb.com and eliteprospects.com for additional sources of information.

Author photo: Andre Ringuette/HHOF-IIHF Images

Illustrations by Bill Dickson

Photo credits:
Andersen: Jonathan Kozub/NHLI via Getty Images
Byfuglien: Len Redkoles/NHLI via Getty Images
Crosby: Gregory Shamus/NHLI via Getty Images
Gaudreau: Derek Leung/Getty Images Sport
Getzlaf: Stephen Dunn/Getty Images Sport
Johnson: Scott Audette/NHLI via Getty Images
Kane: Jonathan Daniel/Getty Images Sport
Karlsson: Andre Ringuette/ National Hockey League
Ovechkin: Scott Iskowitz/NHLI via Getty Images
Price: Richard Wolowicz/Getty Images Sport
Sedin: Jeff Vinnick/NHLI via Getty Images
Seguin: Claus Andersen/Getty Images Sport
Stamkos: Maddie Meyer/Getty Images Sport
Subban: Brian Babineau/NHLI via Getty Images
Tavares: McIsaac/NHLI via Getty Images
Voracek: Elsa/Getty Images Sport
Weber: John Russell/NHLI via Getty Images

www.scholastic.ca

ISBN 978-1-4431-4654-8

6 5 4 3 2 1   Printed in Canada   118   15 16 17 18